D1608781

INVENTING THE
SNOWBOARD

BY CAROLEE LAINE

Published by The Child's World®
1980 Lookout Drive • Mankato, MN 56003-1705
800-599-READ • www.childsworld.com

Acknowledgments
The Child's World®: Mary Berendes, Publishing Director
Red Line Editorial: Design, editorial direction, and production
Photographs ©: iStockphoto, cover, 1, 7, 20; Davor Lovincic/iStockphoto, 4;
budfawcett.com, 8; yulkapopkova/iStockphoto, 11; Alden Pellett/AP Images, 12;
Arno Balzarini/Keystone/AP Images, 15; AP Images, 16; Jean H. Lee/AP Images, 19;
Sampics/Corbis, 21

ISBN 9781634074605

LCCN 2015946286

Printed in the United States of America
Mankato, MN
December, 2015
PA02284

ABOUT THE AUTHOR

Carolee Laine is an educator and children's writer. She has written social
studies textbooks, educational materials, and passages for statewide
assessments. She enjoys learning through researching and writing nonfiction
books for young readers. Carolee lives in the Chicago suburbs.

TABLE OF
CONTENTS

Chapter 1
SURFING ON SNOW..........................5

Chapter 2
COMING UP WITH A GREAT IDEA 9

Chapter 3
CREATING A NEW SPORT 13

Chapter 4
WINNING ACCEPTANCE....................17

Glossary 22
To Learn More 23
Source Notes 24
Index 24

Chapter 1

SURFING ON SNOW

It was Christmas Day 1965. Ten-year-old Wendy Poppen had opened all her presents. So had her five-year old sister, Laurie. The girls' dad, Sherman, took them outside to play. He disappeared into the garage for a few minutes. When he came out, he was holding two skis nailed together to make a wide board. Wendy and Laurie were delighted. They couldn't wait to try it out on the hills around their Michigan home.

Nearly 1 foot (30 cm) of snow had fallen the night before. Wendy stood on the board Sherman had made. Pieces of wood nailed to the board kept her feet from slipping. She held the rope attached to the front end. With one push, she was zooming down a snow-covered hill.

The activity was similar to sledding, but Wendy was standing up. It was also similar to skiing, but there was one ski instead of two. The girls did not know what to call it, but it was fun. Their mom suggested calling it "snurfing" because the activity was like

◄ The original Snurfer was made with wooden skis.

surfing on snow. The boards were called Snurfers. Soon, all of the girls' friends wanted Snurfers, too. "The thing was a big hit and it looked like so much fun," Sherman said.[1]

Snurfing was based on the sports of surfing and skiing. But surfing was possible only in places near an ocean. And skiing required snowy hills or mountains. It was also expensive.

In the 1950s, skateboards had become popular. These boards on wheels made it possible to "surf" on sidewalks. Skateboards were more affordable than skis. But they could not be used in snowy places.

Snurfing may have been similar to surfing, skiing, and skateboarding. But snurfing became a whole new sport. In time, the sport became known as snowboarding. Wendy and Laurie did not know it, but they were two of the first snowboarders. Within their lifetime, snowboarding would become very popular.

By the time Wendy and Laurie Poppen were adults, people ▶ around the world enjoyed snowboarding.

Chapter 2

COMING UP WITH A GREAT IDEA

Sherman Poppen's invention had started out as a toy for children. But by the late 1960s, Poppen had improved his design for the Snurfer. He worked with a company that produced and sold the boards. They became popular with kids all over the country. Soon, adults were joining in the fun.

Poppen was not the only person who came up with this great idea. Other inventors helped create this new winter sport.

Tom Sims was visiting his grandparents in California in the early 1960s. He watched some other kids rolling down the sidewalk on skateboards. That was the first time he had seen skateboards. He begged his dad to buy one for him. From that day on, skateboarding became his favorite sport.

There was just one problem. The Sims family lived in New Jersey. Skateboarding was fine during the warmer months. But

◀ **Tom Sims snowboards in the 1980s.**

during New Jersey winters, sidewalks are covered with snow. Sims hated giving up his favorite activity for a whole season. He was not sure what to do. But soon an opportunity came along.

His seventh-grade teacher gave the class an assignment. Students had to build something out of wood. The project had to be completed before winter break. It would count for their final grades. Sims came up with an idea that could solve his skateboarding problem. And he just might get a good grade, too.

His project was made from a piece of wood that was 3 feet (91 cm) long and 8 inches (20 cm) wide. Sims covered it with carpet on the top and aluminum on the bottom. He added straps on top to hold his feet in place. He called it a skiboard. But would it work?

Sims soon got his chance to find out. After the first snow of the season in December 1963, he took the skiboard to a little hill in front of his home. He stood on the carpeted side of the board. He put his feet in the straps. Then he rode it down the hill. Soon, he was skiboarding down larger hills at a nearby golf course. Sims described his invention as "a skateboard for the snow."[2] Now, he could enjoy his favorite sport year-round. And he got an A+ on his assignment!

▲ A fast turn on the edge of the board is
called a carve.

When Sims grew up, he began a business building
skateboards. After a few years, he started building snowboards,
too. He also used his skateboarding skills to become a
champion snowboarder.

Dimitrije Milovich also built snowboards. He was a surfer on
the East Coast. He went to college in upstate New York. There
was no ocean, but there was plenty of snow. Milovich missed
riding the waves. So he tried surfing down snowy hills standing
on trays from the lunchroom. Then he had a better idea. He
began making snowboards. In 1972, he started a company called
Winterstick. His boards were like surfboards that worked like skis.

In the early 1970s, Snurfers were still the best-known
snowboards on the market. But that was about to change.

Chapter 3
CREATING A NEW SPORT

In the late 1960s, the Snurfing Championships began in Michigan. At first, it was a local event. Over the next few years, it became much bigger. It attracted Snurfers from all over the country. One of them, Jake Burton, changed the sport forever.

Burton had received his first Snurfer when he was 14 years old. He loved snurfing, but he was always messing around with the board. He experimented with ways to make the activity more fun. As an adult, Burton started his own company and began to manufacture boards in 1977.

In 1979, Burton entered the Snurfing Championships in Michigan. But there was a problem. He was not riding a Snurfer. He was riding a Burton Board. The judges decided to divide the contest into two separate events. One was for Snurfers only. The other was for different kinds of boards.

◄ Jake Burton poses with an early model (right) of the Burton Board.

The day of the championships was filled with excitement. Viewers cheered for their favorite Snurfers. Icy air hit the riders' faces as they picked up speed. Some kept their balance and arrived at the end of the slope standing up. Others fell into the snow along the way.

Burton stood at the top of the 312-foot (95-m) slope. He placed his front foot under a rubber strap on his board. His back foot fit into grippers to keep it from sliding. His board was longer and wider than a Snurfer. It had **skegs**, or metal fins, on the back for better control.

Burton rode the slope with style. He showed what a Burton Board was capable of doing. He won the contest for boards other than Snurfers. His prize was $200. He also brought public attention to a new sport. It was not just snurfing anymore. Many other kinds of boards were on the market. The name "Snurfer" belonged to Sherman Poppen. So the other boards were called snowboards. The sport of snowboarding was becoming a big business.

Poppen was still considered the inventor of snowboarding. Milovich left the snowboarding business in the 1980s. But he had helped make the sport more recognizable. His boards had been shown in popular magazines. Burton and Sims became the leaders in making snowboards. They competed against each other. Each tried to build the best snowboard and the best gear. As a result, snowboarding equipment kept getting better. And so did the snowboarders.

▲ By the 2000s, Burton Boards were common in snowboarding competitions.

Chapter 4

WINNING ACCEPTANCE

In the winter of 1982, about 125 snowboarders gathered in Vermont. They were there for a national snowboarding contest. But it was not fancy. The starting gate was a kitchen table. Hay bales marked the end of the run.

A few years later, snowboarding championships were attracting riders from all over the world. Thousands of fans attended. The events were shown on national TV. Snowboarding magazines were widely read. But snowboarders faced a major challenge. They were not allowed in ski **resorts**. They had to use hills in other areas to practice their tricks.

Owners of ski resorts thought snowboarding was too dangerous. They thought skiers would not want to share the slopes with snowboarders. It was a long struggle, but snowboarders slowly began to win respect for their sport. This was a first step toward being allowed in ski areas.

◄ In the 1970s, ski resorts allowed only skiing. Snowboarders were not welcome.

In the mid-1980s, Tom Sims appeared in a popular movie. People who saw the movie found out how exciting snowboarding could be. Around the same time, Jake Burton convinced a major resort in Vermont to accept snowboarders. He also helped make snowboarding popular in Europe. By the 1990s, almost all ski areas welcomed snowboarders.

Not everyone who helped make the sport popular was a snowboarder. Doug Waugh was a farmer. But snowboarding would not be what it is today without his work. Waugh developed a machine that made **half-pipes**. Snowboarders ride these huge U-shapes cut out of snow. Half-pipe tricks are a major event in snowboarding contests.

In 1998, snowboarding was included in the **Winter Olympics** for the first time. From then on, snowboarding became the fastest-growing winter sport. Riders tried to outdo each other.

In 2010, snowboarder Shaun White looked down at the half-pipe lined with cheering fans. It was the Winter Olympics. This was his final run, and he wanted to do something that people would remember. The air was crisp and cold that night. White already had the scores he needed for the gold medal. He did not have to do a trick called the Double McTwist 1260. But

Stratton Mountain Resort in Vermont was one of the first to ▶ allow snowboarders on its slopes.

he decided to go for it. The fans held their breath. White did two flips and three and a half spins.

"I wanted a victory lap that would be remembered," White said.[3] He had shown the world what he could do. He had made history as a two-time gold-medal winner. People said he was one of the greatest snowboarders in history.

PARTS OF A SNOWBOARD

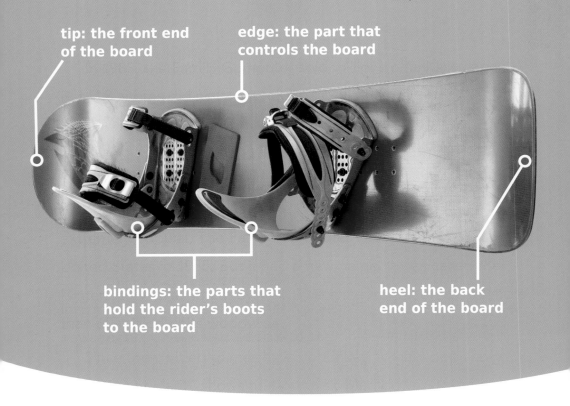

tip: the front end of the board

edge: the part that controls the board

bindings: the parts that hold the rider's boots to the board

heel: the back end of the board

▲ Shaun White does a trick at the 2010
Winter Olympics.

Snowboarding started out as a fun activity for children in the 1960s. More than 50 years later, millions of people were surfing over snowy hills. They were trying out new tricks on half-pipes in hundreds of ski resorts. Snowboarding had become the second-most-popular snow sport in the United States. And it was still growing!

GLOSSARY

aluminum (uh-LOO-mih-num): Aluminum is a lightweight metal that is easy to shape. The aluminum surface helped the snowboard slide easily.

half-pipes (HAF-pyps): Half-pipes are U-shapes cut into piles of snow. Snowboarders do tricks in half-pipes.

resorts (rih-ZORTS): Resorts are places to go for a vacation or for fun. Many ski resorts are closed in summer.

skegs (SKEHGZ): Skegs are metal fins on each side of the back of a snowboard. The skegs on a snowboard give the rider better control.

Winter Olympics (WIN-tur oh-LIM-piks): The Winter Olympics are international sports contests held every four years. Snowboarding became part of the Winter Olympics in 1998.

TO LEARN MORE

Books

Gustaitis, Joseph. *Snowboard.* New York: Crabtree, 2010.

Kenney, Karen L. *Skiing & Snowboarding.* Chicago: Norwood House, 2011.

McClellan, Ray. *Snowboarding.* Minneapolis: Bellwether Media, 2011.

Web Sites

Visit our Web site for links about snowboards: childsworld.com/links

Note to Parents, Teachers, and Librarians: We routinely verify our Web links to make sure they are safe and active sites. So encourage your readers to check them out!

SOURCE NOTES

1. "Sherman Poppen Interview." *Flakezine*. Flake Publications, n.d. Web. 18 Aug. 2015.

2. Dennis McLellan. "Tom Sims Dies at 61; Snowboard Pioneer." *Los Angeles Times*. Los Angeles Times, 15 Sep. 2012. Web. 18 Aug. 2015.

3. "White Defends Men's Halfpipe Title." *ESPN*. ESPN Internet Ventures, 18 Feb. 2010. Web. 18 Aug. 2015.

INDEX

Burton, Jake, 13–14, 18

half-pipe, 18, 21

Milovich, Dimitrije, 11, 14

Poppen, Sherman, 5–6, 9, 14

Sims, Tom, 9–11, 14, 18

skateboarding, 6, 9–11

ski resorts, 17–18, 21

skiboard, 10

Snurfer, 6, 9, 11, 13–14

Snurfing Championships, 13

surfing, 6, 11, 21

Waugh, Doug, 18

White, Shaun, 18, 20

Winter Olympics, 18

Winterstick, 11